POETRY MATTERS

• and poets are important •

Poetry Matters Poems by the 2009•2010
Poetry Month Contest Winners

Edited by Lucinda J. Clark
with Linda Lee Harper

P.R.A. Publishing
P.O. Box 211701
Martinez, Georgia 30917
www.prapublishing.com

Logo designed by LaShondra Mason

Printed in the United States of America

Acknowledgements

We would like to thank Center for Primary Care (CPC) for being our primary sponsor. Special thanks to CPC staff members; Melody Collins, Barry Allison, Lisa Rosier and Gina Behr for coming through year after year. Barry has been our awards program emcee since 2005. He calms down the nervous presenters and brings out the hook for those who forget the time limit on stage. Melody, has come up with many of the marketing and administrative ideas that has kept us growing . Lisa has served as our middle school judge for many years and Gina has been a great help with awards program set-up.

Sharon Schroeder, Deanna Shapiro, Lynette Samuel and Dawn Wilson, served as judges for the two contests showcased in this book. As professional writers, they have added the polish needed to take this project, literally, to the next level.

Linda Lee Harper, served as the anthology's first consultant. As any writer/editor knows publishing a book can be an insane process unless you have a great sounding board. In this case that was Linda Lee. Hope to work with her again soon.

To my husband, Robert and our children Jessica and Xavier. When the idea of a poetry contest was "suggested" about ten years ago, they said they would be there to help. Help was needed to distribute flyers, sort and catalog entries, judge, fold programs, take pictures, stuff gift bags, staff check in tables and just be sounding boards. These guys really came through. And when we were short volunteers, their friends were there too! This anthology nor the contest would be here today, if they had not been there to support the idea until it became a reality. Much love and thanks!

Table of Contents

Middle School • 2009

High School • 2009

Middle School • 2010

High School • 2010

Adult Poets • 2009

Adult Poets • *2010*

Senior Poets • 2009

Senior Poets • 2010

Middle School • *2009*

_____

On This Day

On this day, the sky is red.
With the blood our heroes shed.
On this day, they go home
They've lost all; strength, tears, bone.
On this day, the tires tread
Like a snake, whose skin it has shed.
On this day, the sun goes down
With the silence, of marines who've drowned.
On this eve, our heroes dwell
In the place where earth meets hell.
On this eve, our hearts decline
For our troops who now align
And who'll not return from the night.

Ben Clifford

One in a Million

I gaze out the window at the oak tree
Which has stood for many, long enduring years.

The birds in the nests that fill its heavy, humble branches.
Fly and flutter around as if they have no cares.

Singing high-pitched melodies—God's creatures they are—
They inspire me to listen to my heart's desires.

Everyday I wait for one glance at the blossoming, busy tree;
Its beauty shines through moss-covered arms.

If one tree can shine, in the midst of one million other trees,
Then we should allow God to shine through our moss-laden hearts.

Lillian Brisson

The Warmth of the Earth

The sky is clear and the ground is wet,
The warmth of the earth too cold,
Minutes ago, I was talking to a stranger I had just met,
She was calm sweet, sincere and yet....
The warmth of the earth was too cold.

Stared in awe, like a child I did, for she, was a sight to be seen.
In the window staring back at me, her magnificent eyes glistening,

My mind filled with wondrous thoughts of the places she'd been.
I was humbled to be in the presence of this maiden, this queen,
And she just stared back at me, waiting, watching and listening.
The moment we shared is forever filled with bliss,
Placeless, timeless, never to grow old.
However, I do sometimes miss
That feeling of that snowflake's kiss,
But the warmth of the earth is too cold.

William Kuzia

High School • 2009

———————————————

I wish

Sometimes I wish my life was a musical
Breaking out into random song
Breaking out into random dancing.

Sometimes I wish my life was a TV show
Knowing every line
knowing every phrase.

Sometimes I wish my life was a comedy
Laughing at things that don't make sense
Laughing at jokes that aren't funny.

Sometimes I wish my life was a movie
Being able to call "cut" if I messed up
Being able to redo all my mistakes.

Sometimes I wish my life was a basketball game
Strategizing every move
Strategizing every play.

Sometimes I wish my life was...what it is now.
I can break out into random song
So what if I get funny looks?

I can't know every line,
But I can know some of them, my own.
So what if I don't know how they're going to react?

I can laugh at things that don't make sense.
So what if people think I'm stupid?

I can't yell cut if I mess up,
But I can apologize
So what if people think I'm shallow?

I can strategize my moves
I can think before I act.
So what if I take a second before I speak?

And you know what?
At the end of the day, when I'm lying in bed
Thinking about all the mistakes I made
All the things I've done wrong

I realize
I like my life the way it is
So what about all those what ifs?

Rachel Luoma

Three A.M.

I sit up on my bed at 3 a.m.
Sleeping has become a distant memory for me ever since you blew
Through my life.
I now spend my time thinking about all the things that went
Wrong.

To say I have no regrets would be an understatement.
Why does the thought of you have me up at what is now
3:15 A.M.?
It couldn't have been your smile, truthfully,
I have seen better.
Your eyes were mesmerizing
But
There was never any feeling behind them.
Maybe
It's all the promises you made to me
That are now irrelevant.
The times you promised to change
And then would do the same exact thing
With no remorse.

It is now 3:25 A.M.

And I am the one that can't sleep.
I am not the one who wrecked what we were.
I am not the one who threw us away like yesterday's news.
That was you! You should be tossing and turning at what is now

3:35 A.M.
I refuse to believe that I am awake because of a broken heart,
By the fact, that I was never
In love with you.

3:45 A.M.
Ticks away as I slam my head down in a fit of frustration forcing
My eyes to shut. I refuse
To stay up another minute thinking about your stupid mistakes.

3:55 A.M.
I begin to feel the dreamlike trance that comes upon one when
Sleep arrives.
Thinking I have finally won my raging battle of insomnia.
Only to awake at

4:15 A.M.......

Amber Patterson

Thief

She steps out onto the beige tight rope.
She doesn't teeter.
She doesn't sway.

Instead she balances in perfect harmony
To the words in his voice,
To the beat of his scarlet heart,
To the caress of his alabaster hand.
Never wavering over her feelings
She slowly ambles down the length of taupe
Without looking behind her.
Then a push-

A disastrous plummet into the unforgiving black
Down, down, down.
A spirit escapes her pale lifeless body
Calling for help, accusing him of felony-
Lies, lies, lies

He said he had never fallen for her
But oh how she had tumbled for him.
The specter floats through the pitch black
Like a wispy grey wind.
It watches him walk away from the mess
Through the mass scattered all around,
Sprinkling the dirt with her goodbyes.
While the specter views from above.

The boy rummages about for her torch-red heart.
Brushing the chocolate soil off the front of her peachy throat.
He discovers the object he came for.
Scooping the dead heart into his strong arms.
He returns home to his beige room.
Little by little he opens the door to his attic
Revealing his collection of hearts
Which welcomes its newest member.

Robyn Scott

The Picture

As I work in the field I stop to sigh,
But I am distracted by my little girl's cry.
She cries for me and says the cotton pricked her finger.
So I said, don't worry, daddy will make it better!

I start to head over to my little girl's place
Just to make sure she was safe,
But the overseer angrily stomped and came
So I quickly turned away with shame.

I couldn't help my little girl,
And I watched as she lay there in a whirl.
The sun soon went down and it began to fog.
The overseer called us over to him like a bunch of dogs.

The boss quickly explained
While we all stood there in pain
That he wanted a picture of us weighing cotton.
To show the great productivity of his plantation.

My daughter and I stood there and felt like crying,
And, of course in the picture you could tell our happy faces were lying,
Then all the cotton was weighed
So we were done with our work for the day.

So we went to our shack
And ate a dinner snack.

We went to bed
Knowing what led in the next miserable, repeat-day ahead.

Christina Vazzari
Poem inspired by "Weighing The Cotton", Morris Museum of Art

Middle School • 2010

Feet of a Soldier

For Pop and his amazing, one of a kind wonderful feet.
His shoe size, 13, may make his feet seem large.
But his height, 6'2" makes them perfect.

It may seem strange, but there was a time
When his feet were very,very small.
Those tiny feet of a soldier that were born in Boston fit into little shoes.
They dragged behind him when he crawled.
And balanced his little unsteady body when he learned to walk.

Then his feet got bigger.

The bat made contact with the ball
His feet carried him around the bases.
Soon they pushed the pedals of his first car.

Then his feet got bigger.

His feet carried him to the altar,
When he married his wife Anne.
Soon the sound of little children filled their house.

Then his feet got bigger still.

They carried him onto the plane on his way to Vietnam.
Two times he went as a soldier.
His feet held him up,
standing tall and proud,
In six different ceremonies in which he received six Bronze Stars.

His feet got even bigger.
Soon the sound of little children, seventeen to be exact,
Filled the house again.

Now his feet kick the surface of the water when he tickles in the pool;
They stand on the bottom wearing sandals,
While he uses his radar to find you lurking
Beneath the surface of the ocean.

His feet cannot grow now,
But they can become smaller…
Just run towards him…arms out
And leap into his.
Strong hands lift you into a great big tree frog hug.
You're as tall as a mountain.
On top of the world.
You look down and suddenly,
the feet of this soldier become
Very, very, small.

Annie Fair

Coming Home

The house you lived in.
When you were first born
Warm and cozy, safe from the real world,
That isn't home.

When you moved into the new house
That smelled like fresh paint,
The house that was big enough for you,
Your stuff and more,
That was never home.

When you moved out
Into the small apartment you brought,
Even when you made the final payment,
That wasn't home either.

Time goes on...
You meet your love,
Marry, have kids and move countless times;
Different states, different cities
None of those places were ever home.

But, when you are old and gray,
When everyone comes to visit you all the time so you aren't alone,
When you see God's face and he takes you up to his home,
He takes you home.

Reagan Britton

Reaching

I'm reaching for something.
It's there I can see it;
I'm puzzled what is it?
It's not a goal it's not a dream
I'm getting so close I can just scream
Reaching for something deep within me.
What could it be?

Reaching for strength reaching for courage,
This will take time, so I won't get discouraged.
Reaching for confidence, reaching for pride,
That's something that doesn't need to hide.
Reaching inside to find me,
Reaching for the sky looking for..
Something else
I reached inside to better myself.

AnJanae Wynn

My Picture Book

Nothing feels like hearing the pictures in this old book
Can you hear the peals of laughter from that little girl in the picture?
I can and it's so adorable!
I want to find myself in a picture one day,
Laughing like there's no tomorrow,
Just that moment caught by the flash
And the teasing smile from behind the camera.
There is no worry there,
But, what happens when life comes crashing down?
I run to find my photo book.
And as I look, it feels like the person I lost
Their laughter, it's all gone because so are they.

But, I still have room in here.
And I'll put the people who help me through in there;
When I'm gone, I'll trust you with my picture book.
Hopefully, you'll hear the little girl's laughter; even though she's gone.
I hope you fill it with your own pictures
I hope you hear my laughter from the pictures of me holding you.
My last wish is for you to understand that we hear the laughter
Because we love the people who are caught in that moment in my book.

Jamie Boquist

High School • 2010

_____

Speech of the Masquerade

I speak of the masks I hide behind
It's not just me
It's everyone
It's anyone who wants to be accepted for once in their life.

I speak of the boy who came home crying,
After seventh period ended.
He ran from the teacher-less classroom
Trying his best to block out the teasing,
The constant jokes that now he even sounded like a girl.
He ran straight to his room,
Perched on his bed,
And escaped to his favorite books.
He escapes to lands of the Shire, Hogwarts and Narnia.
Wishing desperately that he could disappear into these fantasy worlds

And before boarding the bus,
He hides his bullet-eaten heart
Covers his once tear, stained face
With a plastered-on smile.
And struts down the hall
Joking and laughing,
Along with everyone else
About the incident of the day before
As if, nothing had ever happened.
A sad teased boy with a painted on smile.

I speak of the girl who sits in the clarinet section
Finally off on a lunch break,
From her shaking hand
Drops her cell phone into her Vera Bradley purse
Just broke up with her boyfriend over the phone.
Tears leak from the sides of her eyes.

She reaches into her bag
For a pair of dark sunglasses
And places them on her face
Covering her puffy eyes.
She pulls her hoodie over her head

Before slumping down in her chair.
From the outside
She looks like everyone else.
From the inside
Her heart has been shattered into a million glass shards.
She acts like it was nothing
Because that's the way she's supposed to act,
The way her friends expect her to act.

I speak of myself,
The girl who wants to show herself.
Show the world that she is something special,
But she 's afraid of what people will think
Afraid they won't like her.
Maybe they'll tease her,
Maybe her friends won't want to be around her anymore,
But she wants to be herself,
She wants to show the world
That she's something more than that quiet little bookworm.
But she's scared,
So she hides herself with her nose in a book
And keeps her thoughts locked up
In a notebook most sacred to her
And never lets anyone glimpse upon her glass heart.
A girl whose voice is still waiting to be heard.

I speak of the face that is shown
When the mask is finally ripped off:
A sad teased boy
A heartbroken girl
An unknown authoress
All part of the masquerade called "Life".

As for me
I now speak and command to be heard.
I abandon my mask
For I no longer need it

So now I speak
For those who toss aside their masks
And show the world
Who we really are
And how we really feel.

Kendall Driscoll

A Fable

As the sun fades in the orange,
I'm reminded of a fable
Of a girl who sat and watched
As the time fell off the table.

As the time fell off the table
As minutes hit the floor,
As they scattered all around
As they drizzled out the door.

And as they drizzled out the door
As she watched them from her seat,
She wondered just how soon again
The two of them would meet.

And when the two would meet again
She'd like to think she'd try
To catch them in her hands
Instead of watching them roll by.

But as she watched them roll
Out the door and down the street,
She knew the time that it would take
For her and time to meet.

As the moon fades in the light
I'm reminded of a fable
Of a girl who sat and watched
As time fell off the table.

Tara Penton

My Guide

Deep in my heart, way deep down
I am a different person from what you see.

Keeping myself hidden from unwanted frowns
I try to be what you want me to be,

It's hard to keep hidden something so prominent,
But I try the best that I can.

The fire there is burning so dominant
But I can't let myself show the way it began,

I cannot show you who I really am
What I really am like.

I'm not sure you would understand:
I'm not sure how I would really strike,

So here goes nothing:
I am bold,
I am passionate
I am fiery,
I am fierce.

I'm a fighter,
I am compassionate,

I'm a lover,
I am me.

There is only one me,
Only one spirit;

Only one life,
Only one love

So, catch me while you can, if this isn't too stunning
I am a free spirit;
I am and nothing can hold me in

So try your hardest to understand me
This persona I keep hidden inside

But it is really me and I cannot condone it
So from now on, my free spirit is my guide.

Rachel Luoma

Spirit of a Soldier

Soldiers possess a uniquely hidden sixth sense
Embracing the secret place of the war zone
Awaiting the summons of nature and suspense
They will heed the call, engulfing the unknown.

Sounds of man's tears streaming silently down
Having haunting memories of the day a life was taken.
Living with constant questions all around
Now looking for truth waiting to awaken.

Countless weary souls are unable to conquer their fear,
Inner-courage and personal strength is what they will need.
However once faced, it will never surface and reappear.
Fear will cease to grow and start to peacefully recede.

Scenic landscapes in the middle of a country's wall
Burdens are eased among the serenity of nature's realm.
Soldiers share their amiable warmth and answer the call.
No longer does the fear of knowing encase them.

The end of one's journey begins the start anew.
Humanity embraces the beauty of peace in passing,
As each dawning day produces fresh morning dew.
The glory in a soldier's spirit is forever enduring and lasting.

Erik Brown

Adult Poets • 2009

_____

Ever Have

Have u ever had that "thing"?

You know, that special thing for that one person.
You know, the one who never knew it, who never got the hints?
Have u ever had something so close to perfection, yet so far from reality?
Something so close to right, yet it was so wrong for so many reasons.
That "thing" that u always dreamed of; the now seeming unattainable.

It was right there u were spoiled by it for so long.
Just havin it made u happy, had u lookin forward
To spendin that time, bein in their presence,
Layin in their arms, close to their heart, feelin the world stop.
Had u smilin at the thought, at every thought...
Of them, of their kiss, their hug, hearin their laugh, seeing their smile
Smelling their scent...

U ever have, that one thing that was so good
U did whatever it took to keep it around?
Didn't wanna admit when the time came it was over.
Didn't wanna let them go, afraid of nothing "like this"
Comin back around again, yet it wasn't right to begin with right?

Funny how we always want what we can't have.
Want what we used to have, can't appreciate
The things we deserve because we're blinded
By the things of the past; from those who didn't deserve us.

Yearning to be loved,wanted, needed and the thought of
The way you think about, maybe even love them.

Ever have that one who could possibly be the one for u?
But because you're stuck in reverse,
Too scared to put your heart in drive
To explore the new path that has been presented to u
Because they were "just right", no other even gets the green light
But when we look back, we see why it was wrong,
We see why we didn't make it work
Then instead of eagerly moving to the next
We hide behind fear of another
Disappointment, too afraid to shift gears.

Have u ever noticed that when u don't look for something
That's when it always appears?
Ever notice that there's always that one u never noticed before
Seeming to notice your every move?
Ever have that one friend who seems to always be at the right place
At the right time?

Always calls or texts at the right time,
Just for some strange reason they got that right time?
Maybe they're waitin for their time,
Because all the time you've been struck...
Stuck in reverse, while they waited in neutral for you to put it in drive.

Ever have that fear you'll never find that happiness again?
Ever have that feeling that you'll always want the unattainable?
Ever have the urge to scream,
So that someone hears u and answers your prayers?
Ever have the dreams and wishful thoughts
That someone would understand?

Sometimes the things we once had,
Are there to remind us of who we are.
Capable of having that, which we deserve more and nothing less.
And that the next one,
Just might be the best one
That we will ever have
And then the others will realize that what they lost
They will never ever have again.

Cierra Baker

On the Search for that Place in Your Life

A good friend stumbled upon it
By chance, she says, through osteoporosis
A messy divorce,woke one morning
To that single ray of enlightenment
Like sun through a slat in the blinds
And she knew she had arrived, the only words
To describe it,
The way you recognize exceptional cello or vintage wine.

Her announcement left me scouring
The house for an unmistakable "X"
That spot where elusive utopia lay
Tangled in a ball of clothes, hunched
Behind a sofa or wedged between
Two hardback books on a shelf.
I cranked open soup cans, a carton of milk
Crossed my fingers as I poured.
Later I ventured outside,
Scattered leaves with my feet,
Rummaged through boxes in the garage
I had not cleaned out In months,
Found everything but,
I suppose, what I might be looking for
But couldn't quite put my finger on.

And now I cannot pass a street sign
Without slowing down, without prowling
Through the overgrown brush for a single arrow
Pointing me there, marked by a tack,
Somewhere on a wall.

It could be the location
I crave will present itself
Several miles from today,
A few hours removed
From my father's death
Cancer, pancreatic, unexpected, early December.

Trudging against the horizontal snow.
My body walking itself
Through a wide canopy of trees
And in the clearing,
The open flap of a tent,
Soft embers of a small fire,
A bundle of warm blankets,
A sense of the familiar
Of someone expecting me.

Kirk Wright

Dreams on Low

Someone came across this dream the other day
So they dusted off the dirt to see what it had to say
It said something to the effect that
"Dreams come true most certainly they do."
This dream has happened to you.

A little further down the page
A little more prophecy came into view,
Quite possibly it's true,
The only thing stopping you —is you.

You are a dream that was too powerful to contain
Why would you maintain a notion that you couldn't gain?
Why not sustain the devotion innate to change?
Do it now
Tomorrow is only a shoulder bicep,
Forearm a palm, one, two, three, four, five fingers away!

Let not these queries inhibit your progress
They were merely to remind you of what you can accomplish.
I hope you have found power in these words you found today.

Please, reset them on the floor
For the next soul through the door
Who dreams no more.

To find the uplifting that has sentenced you to explore
And if you happen across a wayward traveler
Give them the tour!

Allen Champion

I am leading a life

I am leading a life,
Full of seemingly uneventful happenings,
That are potentially life-changing.

My life is as substantial as the Saltine cracker,
Being fed to the starving child somewhere in Africa;
Even the smallest pebbles make a ripple in the pond.

My childhood was tragic
As the woman who peacefully sits in the rocking chair,
Facing the quiet Montana sunrise.

I had a pocket full of pennies
And a need to put them somewhere,
When nowhere seemed right.

I read everything I could,
And knew nothing about everything;
The still perplexing mystery of knowledge,
Eludes even the most studious adventurer.

I thought I was an alien child of the earth,
Wanting to be among the stars;
Childhood dreams burn quick in the atmosphere.

I got caught in the web of a spider reeling in her prey,
The same time I realized the sun always caresses the leaves
Even after the darkest night.

But I still held on to the passing winds so I wouldn't fall.
And now at 18 the earth has grown and the stars have dimmed,
And life is once again for living;
Roots grow deeper, if you let them.
I have heard the sound of rushing water and falling rocks;
I have heard cries and screams, laughter and love,
All essential to the tireless journey meant for the strong,
But walked by the weak.

I know that someday
I can climb those purple mountain majesties
And rest a while in the amber waves of grain,
And as long as I cling to the earth with my bare hands
I know that I will.

I don't know how things come together so perfectly
Or why trees grow so tall,
But they do.
And that is the essence of beauty.

I hate the obvious answers to easy questions
And always hope there are more than words when people talk.
I love the colors of the sunset in June
And the squirrel's perennial search for nuts;
There is comfort in familiarity,
But comfort isn't always comfortable.

I've lost more than I remember
And less than I sometimes think;
Hands don't seem important when you hold them,
But always mean more when they're gone.

I'm looking for something I once knew,
But have since forgotten.
I wish the easily forgotten weren't so hard to remember,
Or that things were neither simple nor complex,
That love was visible in the forgotten everyday,
Or that dandelions weren't weeds;
And somehow I think wishes are a matter of the heart.
And my heart is full of all words and faces and memories.

I once held close;
I still reach out and grasp the passing wind,
Knowing now that even if I let go,
I will not fall.

Thomas Weeks

Adult Poets • 2010

_____

Discovery

I have power.
I am invincible and willful,
Determined to stand my ground,
Unflinching against all invading forces.

My opinion is the law.
Kingdoms conquered
And surrendered,
On a whim.

I am independent;
Standing fast, a lighthouse against the storm
Only curious of the outcome
Never fearing its inevitability.

I have a voice:
Clear and constant, unwavering.
The electric hum of earths rotation
Stiffening against inner adversity.

Or

I am the dandelion.
Dancing on the winds music,
Prisoner to its will,
Longing for stronger roots

Consider, I am fog.
A wispy blanket here and there barely tangible,
Dampness felt more than seen
Hardly noticed, a peripheral minor irritation.

Maybe wet sand,
Steaming through a child's hand,
A mere preoccupation in a hammocked dream of déjà' vu,
A forgotten photo in a bottom drawer.

What if,
I am both,
I am power.
I am the dandelion,
The single pinpoint
Of lantern light.
A tremulous world,
Of my own creation.

All things mixed up,
Confused dear titles.
Mother, daughter, sister
Stranger, friend, enemy.

A melted rainbow
In the creators pot,
Pulsing color
Pushing back,
Caving in.

The rolling reds of aggravation.
A lump of black determination.
Swirls of blue singing of comfort;
A beige dot of inconsequence.

Shards of green choking to live
Sweaty brown of inconsideration,
Constantly evolving,
Seeking, adapting.

I am all of these things
And none of them.

I resist definition,
I am
What I choose to be,
All and nothing.

Me
My greatest discovery!
Just me.

Shannon Jordan

When I Take Command

I often ponder the example set
By those whom I serve under.
Grit my teeth and hold my breath,
When I hear their bellowing thunder
Don't always know the reason
For their harsh, unyielding stand.
But think, "Things will be different,"
When I take command.

Be tactically and technically proficient,
A goal I strive toward
A successful tour of duty,
Will be the true reward
The soldiers will always challenge
"Lead me! If you can."
I will accept that challenge,
When I take command.

I've seen them deep in thought
Of the tasks that they must face,
Send their soldiers off to fight
Somewhere in another place
Decisions of life and death
A challenge for any man
For such reality, I must prepare
When I take command.

Tears they must hold back
A phone call they must make
A senseless tragedy late at night
Someone's heart to break
Although I can't prevent it
That is all in God's own hands

Please Lord let me not face it
When I take command.

The life of the commander
Is challenging, hard, and fun
Demands a positive attitude
Even when under the gun
Although not always popular,
Decisions must be made.
For as soldiers say it's the "Big Bucks"
For which they get paid.

These are the things I pray, oh Lord,
That I will understand.
When I am given the honor,
The honor of command.

Melvin D. Slater

A Triumphant Journey

Life is a journey of epic proportions,
Of many roads and paths to travel on
Success will be determined by packing wisely
And using essentials in a mindful way.

Determination is needed to reach the destination.
Perseverance required to scale obstacles scattered
Along the way
Eyes to see nature's beauty and majesty
Caution to be used as life changes unexpectedly,
As danger is always present, be vigilant against attack.

To reach the finish line
Choose the route taken with care,
Common sense is a trusted friend
The well-traveled paths should be viewed with discernment
The least traveled paths with a healthy dose of courage.

The most important item to take is love.
Love the journey
Love the scenery
Love the obstacles
As they develop character and challenge the spirit within.
Most of all, love others.

The goal is not to reach the destination alone and battered
The goal is to arrive breathless and triumphant
Surrounded by memories of a life,
Well served and work faithfully done.

Ashley Fehrman

Where Are You World

Did you look at me
As I passed you by?
I was the one who looked troubled
The one who sighed.

I'm the one who's job
Just came to an end
The one who realized
I hadn't a friend.

The one who traveled
Through an entire day,
Without one thing to share
Not one thing to say.

I was the one who was beaten
By a husband or a wife,
My body it was bruised
I could not entice.

I was the one
Who's child died in vain.
The one who silently
Hid all her pain.

I was the one whose family
Has gone so far astray
The one who felt hungry
Instead of filled today.

I'm the one whose family
Has been broken and torn
I'm the one who's child
Will never be born.

I'm the one whose father
Turned them away
I'm the on who slept
In a box today.

I'm the one whose mother
Has often abused
I'm the one that people
So often misuse.

I'm the one who sits
Within nursing home walls
I'm the one whose life was taken
Because of a fall.

My face isn't familiar
For your eyes could not see
Your life was too busy
You had somewhere to be.

So let me take one moment
To introduce myself to you
I'm your brother, your sister
I'm the world
How are you?

Leigh Ayers

Senior Poets • 2009

Bird Cage

Dot by meticulous dot
With studied care, the artist stipples her story
In a palette of clumpy colors,
Paying close attention
To weight and placement of every daub.
Each deliberate touch joins with others
Constructing her tale.

From the rug dappled by sun
To the young woman's morning gown,
To torso in corset, as custom demands,
To genteel profile capped by neat coiffure
The door ajar, its window panes
Reflect barely budding trees.

She stands poised there
Looking out into the leafy garden
In her hands the Victorian bird cage
Delicately wrought and ornamented
Held up to the soft wind.

She appears tentative-pondering decision.
Will this be their outing in the fresh breeze or
Persuaded by the air's compelling sweetness,
Will she release her feathered songster
Allow its confined wings to fly away?
And-if she unlocks its cage,
Will she free herself as well?

Gloria Greenbaum
After the painting, " The Bird Cage", by Helen Maria Turner

Dirt Circle

The mountains are the color of fresh bruise.
The warriors at the bus stop
Crouch circled in the hot dirt.
The first warriors wears a flannel shirt
Red sneakers with no laces,
And a necklace made of silver and turquoise
By his grandmother.
He does not like wearing the necklace when he begs.
He drums his backpack with his hand and looks away.
The three warriors sit quietly in the circle
Until the bus from downtown brushes the curb.
The second warrior stands, walks toward toward the people
Palm up as if to check for rain,
And returns to the circle with a few coins.
Now the mountains are the color of ripe grapes.
A cloud builds layer on layer of whiteness
Until it reaches the center of the sun.
The third warrior breaks the circle,
Lays back in the dirt in the dirt, smiling.
Then with one brown finger,
He traces the outline of a white buffalo
He found in the cloud.

B.J. Zmijewski

An Old Horseshoe

It was just an old horseshoe
Nailed above the door
Of my mom's old farm house
In Missouri.

Good luck for some I suppose
But who knows?
It was a hard life
And luck played a part
Faith, hard work and determination
Were what was needed most.

The horseshoe is now
Nailed to my shed.
A piece of time
A piece of mom's past
It watches me with so many stories to tell
But unable in its rusted lifeless form.

Would it bring me luck?
I don't know
But I am glad to glance
Down the path each day
And see it there.

Watching me,
Collecting one more story
And another layer of rust
As it hangs there.

Waiting perhaps for my son
Or daughter to do the same
When it is their time to
Take down the old horseshoe
Take it to a new home
Where it will watch over them
Perhaps lucky,
A piece of family history, all the same.

Roger Brock

Flashback Vietnam

Yellow-red flowers that blossom at night,
Stark lines of red in the darkness.

Crumpled forms clad in green and in black,
Lifeless hands reaching for attention.

Restless sleep, peopled with shifting ghosts
Thoughts of days no longer existing.

Demons, springing from the mind, killing all sleep
A return to years of the past.

Though bridges are burned and new beginning sought.
For each day's calm, there is still a night.
And fear.

D.C. Skinner

Time

He watches the drops drip, drip, filling his veins ever so slowly
With hopes and dreams—another tomorrow may bring
Praying for the precious time this potion might give him
More time—time to just sit awhile with his "Honey"
Time-to enjoy the lives he gave to the world
Time-to savor all the rewards that life has given him
Maybe tend to his gardens and feathered friends.

Time-to do all the things he once just dreamed about
Reading his bible daily for words of strength and salvation
Inspiring him with the tenacity to endure the constant pain
He fights this monster that has invaded his once strong body
Battling these demons seeking to plant seeds-of fear and despair.
Using his faith and the will to live as his only weapons
Determined against all odds to defeat this goliath
To fight the fight; to win the battle
He is the bravest of warriors
He is our Hero!

His body is beginning to fail him and he is getting so tired,
Tired of the never-ending pain struggling to just breathe.
This goliath has taken over his body, but never his spirit.

His faith has grown stronger with each passing day.
He's ready to go home and meet his blessed Savior.
Asking sweet Jesus to give him a garden in heaven,
A garden to grow beautiful roses for his sweetheart
When her time on earth is over and she will join him.

Yesterday he watched the snow slowly falling to the ground.
Covering the sleeping trees and earth with its pure white blanket
Reminding him that sweet Jesus has washed away his mortal sins
Never succumbing to despair, or surrendering to the enemy.

Instead he has placed his earthly life in his saviors hands.
Who blesses him with precious time to spend with his love ones,
He's won the greatest battle of his life-saving his eternal soul,
He's fought the fight and conquered the enemy.

He is the bravest of warriors!

Sarah Bailey

Senior Poets • 2010

Sonnet to a Sculler

At first light, I open the bedroom blinds
Onto the gray Savannah River
Art spreads out below.

A Thomas Eakins-Max Schmitt in a Single Scull
In his sleek, yellow shell
Muscles pulling with steadfast rhythm
Against the willful current,
The rower masters the taskmaster waters.

I envy you out there in the freshness
The rivery tang skimming your senses.
I savor the strength of your sturdy back and limbs
Youthful energy carrying the scull upriver.
You may think birds your only watchers
But I too share this pure moment.

Gloria Greenbaum

Mother and Child Mary Cassat

I will keep somewhere in me
The touch and smell of you.
Fresh from a bath
Moist soapiness
Powdered roses
Sitting in damp haired splendor
On white linen throne.

There we will always have time,
For oranges and hot tea
From shell thin china cups
And there,
I will always keep the child
You will never be again.

B.K. Zmijewski

She sits in her room waiting

She sits in her room waiting
For anything really, something interesting
A smiling face, another voice.

Two years seems like a long time,
But many have been here a lot longer
At the Blue Springs Nursing Home.

It's a long time between breakfast and lunch;
Take a nap they say, watch some tv.
She used to be so busy,
First raising kids forever it seemed,
Proud to say she put them through school,
Then they moved away and had their own kids.

Yes, they used to visit twice a year
To see how she was doing
And later for her to see the grandkids.
Life flies by so fast.
And then, you are in a rocker at Blue Springs.
Lost her husband of 50 years some time ago.

Things started going downhill fast after that;
Lonliness is a silent killer.
No one to fill that special void,
Companionship.

Tried to hang onto the old homestead for a while
Living alone,
So many memories, who would want to leave?

Hard when the mind starts to go, however
Little things at first,
Then ones that really matter.
Did I take my medicine this morning?
And just what day is it really?
Have I eaten yet today?

Time to go, Mom
The family says:
You can't live here anymore by yourself.

We'll get you somewhere safe
With others like yourself,
You'll have new friends.

It never will be the same, however:
The good old days are gone now
The house sold in a week they tell me.

So get with the program.
Let them fuss over you
It's their turn now, they say.

Life takes so many turns
You're near the end
But you're also back at the beginning,
Come over, Mom
Wear that nice pink outfit we got you,
I guess Mable will help me get ready.

Hope my lunch group doesn't worry about me
Did she "kick the bucket"? they'll ask.
What is her name again? Nice lady.

Later she sits in her room again waiting.
Take a nap before dinner I guess,
Chicken strips tonight at Blue Springs.

Roger Brock

Grands of the Divorced, Divorced

Step into my world of step-grandparent
Inherent, non-transparent, aberrant.
Twice removed since they're yours from before us
And hers from a previous muss and fuss.

Add in the Exes who never will share
Also refusing to ever play fair.
Hog tied between us and them; no splitting,
No say; nothing doesn't seem quite fitting.

Such a simple thing; coming for a swim,
All details to work out made it quite grim.
An unwillingness to negotiate,
Makes us unable to associate.

Such a little hope for understanding,
Another generational stranding.
Grand losers of attention; affection,
Sweet and innocent with no intention.

Grands, undeserving of isolation,
Imposed upon strictly by relation.
Someday they might figure out the riddle,
So unfair to put them in the middle.

Until they grow to work out the puzzle
I'll wait, seething behind my step-muzzle.

Janis Krauss

www.ingramcontent.com/pod-product-compliance
Lightning Source LLC
Chambersburg PA
CBHW020951030426
42339CB00004B/51